Overcoming Divorce: How to maneuver Divorce from ruining your marriage

John L. Carl

-

Table of contents

-

Foreword

It has been postulated too many times that men and women are radically opposed creatures. The idea goes on to argue that there are fundamentally distinct things that drive both these genders, and there are different things that they are seeking. That is the reason men and women act and behave in fundamentally different ways.

Now, although the reality is that nature itself has ordered us to be different, which means our actions are indicative of the gender that we belong to, it is also a dismal fact that this may bring a lot of issues.

There are various cases in which men and women do not understand one other, owing to which there are conflicts and fights between the two, even leading to grave actions such as breakups and divorce.

Now I desire to inform you, yes! You can take back the love of your life! Whatever how tenacious the resistance, regardless

-

of how distant this person could be from you, regardless of how dismal your situation of things looks!

I'll teach you the tried and true and tested tactics in this e-book which you can understand and implement instantly to strengthen your love connection and even your marriage!

-

Chapter 1:The Basics
Synopsis

There are some fairly weighty and awful figures concerning relationships that have not worked out, yet it is true that if just a little more effort and understanding were utilized, many relationships may have worked extremely well.

The purpose of this eBook is to explain what repairs may have been feasible in relationships that soured down and to highlight that with some more attentive work, many of our relationships could be diverted correctly.

This e-Book tells you that men and women are inherently different and we need to acknowledge and embrace these differences. We need to recognize that there are various things that we search for in life, and even in a relationship, there are distinct things that a man and a woman look for in each other. If this one basic rule of nature is kept in mind, then both genders would be able to live in greater peace with each other.

-

Realizing our diversity, we would be in better stead to create a cohesive whole.

The Basics

It takes time and it takes work, but, most importantly, it requires a tremendous degree of maturity and understanding. If we accept these differences in our spouses, we will have more meaningful relationships. With this eBook, we are not attempting to advise you to alter what nature has formed you as—that is not going to happen—but it is vital to know that your spouse is a different person. They don't have to enjoy the same things that you do and say the same things that you express.

At the same time, most of the things that we describe as selfish and inconsiderate in our relationships, are very different from what they look. These things are nothing but the essential qualities of such folks. They are fashioned to act in that certain way. If a guy forgets his wife's birthday, it is not because he does not care for her—it is because nature has intended for him to concentrate on one task at a time.

-

Maybe he was simply too engaged with something else, his attention was physiologically diverted to that work totally, and he messed up. Or, when a woman spends too much time looking after herself, the man should not think that she is being vain. Nature has developed women in such a manner that they prefer to take care of their beauty.

This is what we have to comprehend and accept. Instead of transforming the world into a battle zone full of animosity between the sexes, it is vital to comprehend the diametrical distinctions between the two genders and live in peace. We are designed to be different. It is time to embrace it and live in peace.
In this eBook, you are going to see the numerous ways in which man and woman are intended to be distinct. You are going to discover how to figure out these differences in your relationship and what you should do so that there is no reason for the dispute.
We will propose you keep a record of

-

your relationship, a journal that you will develop and update in conversation with your spouse. You will be able to vent out your sentiments in this notebook and you will be able to grasp how your spouse is disposed of as well. You will discover that simply the effort of keeping this notebook will go a long way in enabling your relationship to develop.
Vital and basic tenets you have to grasp first off if you, really, honestly desire to win back the one you love and maintain your marriage!
Mankind only wants what they don't have.
Humans baulk things which command or constrain them.
Humans adore themselves to a greater degree than anything else.

In the first place, you have to study and remember the following highly fundamental commandments of mortal nature. To a certain degree, these rules apply to anyone, including you and me!

Critical items you must not do if you seriously desire to recover your mate or

-

maintain your marriage don't indicate that you're hungry for your spouse’s or mate’s existence.

Regardless of how much you desire your partner or your spouse to stay by your side, or to be back with you, more hungry and holding on will just make that person even more exhausted and fed up with seeing you or making up with you.

Rather, establish the mental attitude, habit and behaviour such that you don't need that person to be nearby for your enjoyment or pleasure. You don't need someone else’s presence or approval to experience pleasure and tranquillity.

If you find out how to create this form of mental attitude and habit, you'll realize that your companion will be the one who will grow afraid! They will grow terrified of losing you!
Think of this: human beings tend to crave what they don't truly have!

If your companion or husband is seeing

-

anybody other than you, don't prohibit them from seeing other people! Have a rival around?
Here's what you have to do. Don't stop your partner from seeing others. If you sound off, moan, and complain, I can assure you, the more they'll desire to see the other person!

How come? They can't bear your sounding off, yammering, and nagging! If you intend to block someone from getting something that they desire, all the more they'll crave it! Humans tend to desire what they don't have.

So, if you try to prohibit them from seeing a different person, all the more they'll want to be with that individual! To them, it'll be a wonderful challenge if you try to stop them.

If they ever win that person, they'll feel victorious about it! And guess what, you're the one confronting them that they won't have what they seek! Remember, struggling to bring back the one you love virtually ensures your

-

defeat.

So, what you have got to do is to allow them freedom of choice! Let them believe that you're the better person to be around than your competitors since you appreciate their freedom and their alternatives!

Don't limit your companion or your spouse. Human beings tend to baulk objects or others that command or constrain them!

Respect your mate's choices or wants to do anything he/she chooses to do throughout a given day or during a specific period.

If he/she chooses to go out with someone else today, leave them alone! If he/she doesn't desire to see you today, let them leave!

The more you don't offer them your tending, guess what, they'll want you are tending back! They'll begin desiring it! And they'll eagerly want it back.

-

The more you supply them attention, the more they'll sense that you want to command them, to constrain them, and the outcome is, they'll baulk it, they'll struggle back! This will merely ruin the bond between the 2 of you.

-

Chapter 2:Then And Now

Synopsis

Very few individuals may be entirely content with their life nowadays. Surely, most lives nowadays are covered by difficulties such as mistrust among couples, arguments over little concerns, suspicions, ill will and even hate. Relationships are continuously souring all around us, and most times, we believe that nothing can be done about it. We surrender ourselves by claiming that it was supposed to be that way.

Life was entirely different in the good old days, at least on the look of it. We weren't so technologically savvy back then and maybe we paid more weight to our ties than we do now. Man needed women and women needed men more than they do today—that is a reality.

The View

The forms our relationships are adopting right now are just awful. 1 in 2 marriages

-

are ending up in a split or a divorce. The levels of hatred are undoubtedly growing, and this is surely no good.

Why is this happening? What is it that we are failing to see? Despite making a fanatical commitment at the start of our relationship, in the heydays as you may call it, what occurs that makes the connection so profoundly irreparable?

Certainly, the fault rests in one of the couples or both. There are some pretty fundamental things that we are simply losing out on. We are not investing the time to comprehend that men and women are fundamentally different sorts of creatures and that the only way to live effectively in peace is by knowing each other thoroughly.

If you believe it is too tough to attain, you need to think again. You need to recognize that the situation is not all as gloomy as it looks. There is only one link in this chain, one solitary strand, that we are missing out on. If we merely notice this one missing connection and accept it, we will be able to accomplish much better with our life.

That is what it is all about—mutual understanding and acceptance. That is what we need to learn.

And, sure, in this chapter, we begin establishing the record of your relationships that will help salvage your rocking relationship boat. This is your reference point and your guide, the location where you feel your fumbling connection starting to take root once more.

We see this very common scenario in the world around us today... maybe in our own lives too.

It is someone's wedding day. They look into each other's eyes and vow to be together "until death do them part". Standing in front of the marriage celebrant it is difficult to imagine how the two could ever not feel so in love as they do today.
Yet 5, 10, or 15 years later they are

-

standing in front of a judge and this time they are told they are divorced. It is not quite the fairy tale conclusion they had envisioned all those years ago.

This situation is a reality for almost 50% of couples who are married. While the duration of the relationship may be varied across couples, and there are other causes for divorce, the truth is, that over half of all marriages will end in divorce. The statistics are worse for remarriages.

It is a bleak image, and maybe you are feeling dejected thinking about what hope your marriage or relationship has in the face of such statistics. The beautiful thing about statistics is that there are positive as well as poor statistics and other data suggest that if a couple can

work over the challenges in their relationship; they might perhaps connect more than ever and go on to enjoy an even greater relationship.
Why is all this happening? Ultimately, it

-

is our beliefs of what constitutes a healthy relationship and our expectations of our spouse, which produce the tension in the marriage.

As we learn to understand why we have these expectations and how to deal with them, we may look at our relationships with fresh eyes and enjoy them for what they are, rather than for what they are not, With this understanding, all relationships possibly can progress ahead.

Our capacity to relate to one another has grown during our lives. We learn through watching the society we grew up in and via our life experiences. As children, we observe our parents and we notice how they connect.

We connect with our siblings and this helps our understanding of how individuals in intimate relationships interact with one other. We learn via chatting with our friends and frequently compare and contrast their experiences with our own. As we focus on what

-

affects the way we engage with people and why it does this, we uncover the key to starting the repair of a good relationship.

Here are a handful of practical actions that may improve the process. Try to accomplish them jointly as a pair.

Reflect on who you are and what has impacted your opinions on life and relationships. Take a day or two to truly think carefully about this and ask your spouse the same questions. Compare their opinions with yours.

Use a notebook to write down major occurrences in your relationship each day and what experiences led them to occur and what your expectations were that produced that let down. These events go a long way in cementing your ties. Even though you feel that you are moving away if you simply chance to read about these experiences in your notebook, you will remember those great days you had together and maybe you will have a change of heart. You will

-

attempt to patch up the relationship again. You would want to be together again to experience those joyful days, and somewhere deep within, you will receive the assurance that the situation is not as gloomy as it looks on the outside.

Chances are that your companion is contemplating as well. Since the love you started with was pretty strong and resolute, your spouse is not likely to want to peter it down either. Sit together and ponder. Maybe a solution will emerge out of the entire morass. Maybe you will want to be together for life once again, just as you committed to each other during that marriage.

But things have changed. We have grown more mechanical, and more materialistic. Our lives aren't as easy as they were previously. Our commitments of the day aren't split simply into work time and family time. Many more items fight for our attention each day.

Still, the fundamental norms that were

set back then are still extremely popular. Gender roles were imposed on men and women back then, all those years ago, and they persist. Woman lib nevertheless, there are still gender roles that remain widespread. And this is more typically observed when individuals are in a relationship.

Until recently, people usually married for life with one and occasionally in polygamous communities several spouses. Fifty years ago when individuals divorced, they typically faced allegations and lost lifetime friendships. Today, it is possible that many of them in our circle of acquaintances are divorced and may even have remarried to new partners.

If we go back even farther to the days when our ancestors were hunters and gatherers, we find an entirely different scenario from what is the reality for most couples today. History has shown us that our ancestors were a mainly hunting and gathering society. Men would go and hunt for food while women

-

gathered mostly seeds and berries surrounding their houses.

They relied on each other for the provision of everything material, but for the most part, they did not receive a lot of direct emotional

assistance from each other. Instead, males established a friendship with the guys they hunted with, while the women spent much of their time with each other, helping care for children and preparing meals. Ladies frequently obtained the emotional support they needed from the women they worked with each day.

This trend was maintained into the 20th century. Although the sort of jobs that men and women conducted changed considerably, the gender roles remained largely the same. The male would go out to work and the lady would remain at home. This situation is not just generally true in "western" civilization; research of other foreign cultures shows comparable patterns.

-

During the 20th century, established positions started to alter. Perhaps the world wars provided a necessity for women to work outside the house, but women began to take on traditionally masculine vocations. In certain cases, women made more money than males did. Some males even started to remain at home and care for the children. Traditional gender roles started to alter, women pushed for equal rights and in a few instances, men began opting to remain home, and care for their children and house while their wives worked.

The response of men and women to this tendency is fodder for many books and audio presentations on how this transformation has altered the way men and women connect. The common theme that appears to be emerging from all studies and research is that men will be men and women will be women.

It seems that no matter how much civilization is growing, certain things

-

stay the same. There is a consistency in the way males look at circumstances and deal with them and the way that women look at situations and deal with them. The gender-specific requirements of both men and women have altered little from the time of our forefathers and most difficulties come when those were disregarded Controversial concepts may appear to be, but vital to ponder about regardless.

You and your companion may choose to ponder on this notion in your diaries. Knowing how to identify and meet your personal own needs is the first step in healing a broken relationship.

-

Chapter 3:Know The Differences

Synopsis

Men and women comprehend emotion, communication, sexuality, faithfulness, work and income because of the way they were socialized and because they've been influenced by their own parents' perceptual experiences. They bring these ideas to the marriage and therefore have their baggage of notions regarding what is passable and intolerable in a union, what they have to provide their mate and what to anticipate in return.

There is a constant power struggle between the two human genders on this planet. This is not different from the competition, in which each gender wants to impress upon the other that they are better than the other.

This is a very sorry state of affairs. If instead of all these discords, the two genders would live together in harmony, the world would become a more harmonious place.

-

The Differences

You can see this in the dissimilar ways men and women pick a partner:
Women attack love as informed consumers...they kick the tires, see under the hood, run the engine, and check out the mileage. Women enjoy love, however being practical-minded, is not enough to ignore likely shortcomings. Handsomeness and romantic love interest a woman, but in thinking about likely suitors, a woman likewise views the practical, like a wooer's economical prospect, emotional stableness, trustworthiness, and what sort of father he will be.

Despite a reputation for practicality, male persons come away as hopeless romantics. They're much more prone to fall topsy-turvily in love and likewise more prone to idealize the target of their fondness.

If the bodywork is great and the grillwork pretty, frequently a man will

-

purchase on-the-scene, no questions asked. It requires practice to learn that gender differences don't represent menaces to a marriage, merely a cause for celebration and a chance to enlarge a person's area of experience.

Attempt to remember that your companion isn't your reflection. In a loving, healthy relationship, individuality and separateness are healthful notions that each mate must strive on.

Don't sweat the small things is certainly one suggestion that doesn't forever work for marriage, since it's vital to monitor the minor stuff if the marriage were to survive. Most of the important work in relationships is coming about in more quiet times in littler locations.
Illustrations would be:

Putting off bringing up the faulty garage door when your spouse is trying to fulfil a deadline and needs to focus on his assignment for a couple of hours.

-

Assisting the children and keeping them away from the kitchen while your wife cooks dinner.

Offering to collect your hubby's clothes from the cleaners since he forgot to do it yesterday.

Fill the automobile tank if you know that your spouse needs to travel out of town on a client appointment.

Bringing your wife dancing since she's always liked to dance even though you've two left feet and have always loathed it.

One thorn in a marriage is money. Chances are married folks have their methods of spending and putting down cash. If both husband and wife make a similar income, agree on how to share the household costs before married so neither one feels cheated or disadvantaged financially.

When it was all fine to expect him to pay for dinner and the movies while you were going out, marriage asks for a true

-

economic relationship. Or, if you recognize that your spouse is very

As opposed to meaningless shopping flings, endeavour to cut down your purchasing excursions and focus on your needs rather than on your desires.

Don't forget to speak about your investment preferences and endeavour to stay within a budget and a savings strategy.

Work at keeping your mate perked up mentally. If there's anything that grinds, it's a lady who continually talks about what's on sale and a guy who knows nothing but what teams made it to the playoffs this year. Retrospect to romance days when both of you could converse until the wee hours of the morning as you were interested in what each of you did in the workplace that day, in that book or film etc.

Enrich one another with your life and vicarious experiences. Let the other know that you have a quest in life and

-

what it has to give, and make every attempt not to be a boring spouse by reading more, trying out more, and living more.

A lot of people declare that children put a damper on the connection. Who has time for passion and love when the children are screaming their hearts out or having one hundred-five-degree fever? Or when revenue needs to be scrounged up to pay for teeth?

Raising kids may make us into irritable, stressed-out creatures thus if hiring a sitter overnight won't affect the monthly budget, do so

and disappear – just the two of you. But don't use that time away from children to sound off regarding each other's behaviours or to bring up old mishaps! Rather than considering marriage blessed with raised peaks or burdened with shattered points, look at it instead as a sequence of markers.

Landmarks have to be considered as an

-

opportunity to make a marriage stronger and more rewarding. These milestones become obvious in mid-life when couples have established a higher sense of time limitations and an urgency in their drive to get the most out of their partnership and their lives.
The mid-life years are an intrinsic period for contemplations: couples now have the luxury of being able to recognize where they've been, where they are and where they aspire to go.

Provide credit where it's due, be generous with consideration and be honest in your compliments. Do you sometimes find yourself hoping that your partner would congratulate you? A lot of couples feel that once they settle into their partnership, the esteem or nice compliments are not as common as when they were going out. Giving credit where it's due and being real about your compliments go a long way toward establishing wellness in a marriage.

If you notice that your wife works regularly on the treadmill to avoid

-

weight, did you ever imagine that she's likely doing this to please you? Stating something like, "You're so diligent in your endeavours to reach your objectives, I'm happy for you" will add to her

self-assurance and confirm her stance that she's doing something suitable and that you appreciate it.

If your spouse is adept at crunching numbers, thank him for his efforts in rapid computation. "You're astounding with numbers" will offer him a sensation of pride, and he will feel important to you. Sure a lot of authorities and marriage counsellors will disagree in view on how to preserve a marriage, but they all agree on the following key Components of a strong marriage – just the words and the manner they're delivered are different.

We Are Designed to Be Different!

Men and women have been equated as being citizens of two distinct worlds in a

-

popular series of novels now on the market. The idea of the author is that despite popular, current thinking men and women are different. In truth, they do have a propensity to think and behave in a distinct manner depending on whether we are male or female.

This is because men and women are built differently! Some of the disputes that occur inside a relationship are the consequence of neither member of the pair recognizing this truth. Without getting overly scientific, the practical effects of these variances are that men and women react differently to the same scenario.

This is not because either member is indifferent, forgetful or in some way not responsive to the requirements of their spouse, it simply means that in many circumstances they are unable of being any different, just because this is a gender-specific condition and not a personal one.

Where the Power Struggle Begins and How to End It

Understanding that a male will always want to solve an issue rather than speak about it and a woman will always want to talk it out to solve it is vital. Women sometimes claim men don't want to listen to them speak about their difficulties, while their quiet husbands often wish that women would stop talking about the problem so they can fix it.

The architecture of the male brain is specialized to concentrate on one task at a time and accomplish that job. The neurological system in his brain is "wired" so that he can notice a problem, find out how to remedy the issue and then fix it. His brain equips a guy with the capacity to think logically, work effectively with numbers and generally perform complicated jobs.

Women, on the other hand, have a brain that is "wired" to multitask successfully. Women tend to be able to do the

-

laundry, prepare meals, and care for the children at the same time.

When a woman asks her husband to do anything when his mind is busy and his concentration is elsewhere at the moment, he is apt to

forget her request, although this is inadvertent on his side. He did forget, not because he does not love her enough to carry out the request, but because his mind was in doing something else at the time, she made the request.

Recognizing that there are fundamental physiological differences (including hormonal ones) that control the behaviour of men and women is a vital step in understanding that our partner's failure to fulfil our expectations are frequently unintentional. Once we can accept it, we may see the acts of our partners from another viewpoint.

For Your Journals

Discuss a recent misunderstanding you

-

and your partner experienced with eachother. Write about the differences between men and women and think about how your partner's behaviour in that circumstance that hurt you may have been representative of the disparities between genders rather than anything personal they are "doing wrong"

-

Chapter 4:Mind Your Tongue Synopsis

Things you utterly must not state if you truly wish to change the mind of your mate.

Watch What You Say

If you wish to change the mind of your spouse or mate concerning anything, you have to not say "But I love you..." I can tell you, that stating that and stressing how much you love them isn't going to get them to change their mind.

When you state "But I love you..." you are in reality telling your mate that you wish him/her to do something your style! Not his/her style.

Recall that "human beings tend to love themselves to a higher degree than anything else!" When you state "I love you..." you are in reality loving yourself more. You wish your spouse to do things which will gratify your ego, thus you wish your spouse to do things your way.

-

And your spouse recognizes it! He/She is not going to alter his/her mind simply because you tell them “I love you...”

If you wish your spouse to do particular things your way, you have to not say to your partner “But I've done this and this for you...”

Prevent stirring up the past about what you've done for him or her. The past is already deceased. Stressing how much you've done for your spouse will only tell him/her that he/she has to do stuff your way because that's the price they have to ante up for all that you've helped them do in the past.

The more you state this, the more your mate will wish to drift apart from you or leave you. He or she will be too frightened to be with you as they know their motion is restricted by how much they may repay you.
So, at any expense, prevent giving them the feeling that they have to ante up a price simply to be with you! No one on this Earth likes to be commanded or

restricted by another individual!

Prevent stating things like “But it’s your duty....”

Your mate won't like to be tied down by duty or obligations. When it bears on a relationship, there can be rules. Love is unconditional. By\sStressing too much on duty, you're going to turn your mate off.

He or she won't desire to be with someone who wishes to impose rules and ordinances on them. So, it is your job and obligation to see that you give your spouse no excuse to leave you for some other individual.

So, what precisely must you say if you wish to alter the mind of your spouse to make them accomplish things your way, or view things your way?

First of all, stress the strong points if they view things your way. Let them recognize the Advantages and benefits of executing and viewing things your way.

-

Provide them with clear-cut explanations.

Second, remember your mate isn't concerned about what other people want. He or she isn't worried about what you wish. He/she is more interested in what he/she wants and what he/she may receive. A lot of times, they're not against your thoughts, or whatever it is you need, but they're really against your pushing aside their freedom of choice.

So, provide them with what they desire. Provide them freedom of choice. Let them know they have the freedom to choose what they wish to believe in or what they don't wish to believe in. And let them know they have the freedom to decide what they wish to do, and what they wish not to do.

The magic words you can tell them are “Yes! I comprehend what you're saying. Why don't you try it /do it...”

“Yes” is the magic word which unites you

and your partner right away.

“I comprehend...” demonstrates you're with your partner, you're hearing them out, and you honour their decision.

“Why don't you try it / do it ...” tells them you back their decision or choice, even though you're not in favour of it.

If you're a competitor, always remember, that the individual who may give your mate more freedom of choice will most likely be the one your mate wishes to be with most.

If you bear all the above precepts in mind, you're likely to have more success in altering your mate's mind and making them accomplish things your way.

Chapter 5:Thriving

Synopsis

Friends are evermore. Even if we move out of town or take residency overseas, we keep our friendships. We don't divorce our pals only because of a misreading, so if we addressed our spouse as a loving buddy, we likely won't ever need a divorce lawyer and carry out then horrible exercise of divorce.

There is substantial scientific proof in what we say—the difference between man and woman is not simply a question of guesswork; there is an actual hormonal cause for it. While males are led by the powerful testosterone hormone—a hormone that provides a type of an aggressive edge—women are guided by the gentler oxytocin hormone, which urges them to give and accept love and care.

So, it is not merely a surface difference that the two sexes on our planet share. There is much more. The difference

-

extends deep within; it deals with the hormonal constitution of the two genders. That's what makes us so distinct.

If we want to live on this planet, we will scarcely be able to achieve so by living in isolation and focusing on our own selfish goals.

Changing It

When two individuals in a relationship are under stress, tiny things frequently become huge concerns. Situations that at one time would have been potentially missed are now added to the list of things that the spouse is doing wrong.

Once a relationship reaches this stage, it is extremely difficult for one or both parties to appreciate the excellent things their partner may provide them and the relationship.

Men and women are motivated by their hormones. Testosterone the male sex hormone, and oxytocin, the female sex

-

hormone both play incredibly crucial roles in the way men and women behave and respond. Testosterone generates a drive in males to protect and provide for their spouses.

Oxytocin promotes a strong yearning in women to nurture and care for others.
Adequate amounts of these hormones are required to induce a sense of wellness and happiness. When both spouses have strong hormone levels, they cope with life and their relationships constructively. When the hormone levels are lowered, stress levels are heightened, leading to a higher chance of conflict within the partnership.

When couples had established roles, it was easier for the pair to live their lives with these hormones running normally. The male in the partnership would go to work and generate enough money to maintain his family with a respectable lifestyle and all their necessities. The lady in the partnership would remain home and care for her family. When

-

partners are in a healthy relationship and know and react to each

other's needs physiologically, emotionally and socially, these hormones are created in increasing amounts.

Society and circumstances have affected the way we do things.
Often, the male is no longer the primary provider and his wife may have a career, and yet still feel the need to nurture and care for her family. Both of these scenarios produce stress. The guy no longer believes his wife has the same need for his supply, something that would push him to achieve in the past.
The lady feels annoyed she still frequently needs to go home and do most of the work around the house since her husband appears to prefer to go home and sit and read the newspaper or watch the television.

Testosterone and oxytocin are created differently in each partner and if couples realize this, it will assist transform the

-

way they interpret this circumstance. In this circumstance, each member of the pair is automatically doing what is required for them to replenish their hormone levels.
At the end of the day, both had come home with low hormone levels. To boost her levels the lady has to nurture and care and give and receive love to promote oxytocin production.

Relaxation is his approach to raising his hormonal levels.
Spend some time pondering all your partner's great traits. Write them down in your notebook and spend some time every day to read them and ponder how much your spouse provides to your life.
Read more about the way our hormones impact our behaviour and reflect on this in your notebook.

Since love is less durable and friendship more long-lasting, every exertion must be made to make our companion isn't just a lover and a partner, but as well a friend. Friendship is an evident expression of matureness.

-

Marriage is a task greater than life and maybe a source of stress or sound delight. Only if we transform those concerns and pleasures into building bricks for a long relationship may we state that we've followed the solid route to a union created in heaven.
If there's actual camaraderie between husband and wife, the marriage avoids ending up on the rocks. Rather it becomes a rock-hard marriage where no person or situation may throw it asunder.

Friendship in a relationship suggests that the union will be noteworthy with memories of fun and humour because didn't we choose those friends who made us laugh the most? Friendship likewise signifies free and honest communication; a no holds barred sort of coupling where our comfort level with our partner extends beyond a hundred per cent, assured that what we state and how we say it won't be branded or taken in a harmful light.
The friendship between spouses provides pleasant emotions of goodwill

-

and constancy. Our spouse - our buddy – has our problems at heart, won't cheat on us and will be our most faithful supporter.

Friendship also makes mates stronger; this durability is fostered by the joy of shared past, nostalgia and dreams for the future.

Romance is a terrific thing, and we may employ heaps of it when our partnerships go difficult. But mature friends are mindful that passion may be a hurdle to friendship. How come? As romance blots away the darker half of our existence - our problems, anxieties, and insecurities. Yet, it's those worries, concerns and uncertainties that by nature pull us to our buddy.

Familiarity doesn't create contempt. It generates content. A sensation of contentment connects with happiness, warmth, and strong certainty. Partaking in life together in love and friendship makes for a book that's richer and denser in shared history and substance.

If you were to ask a pleased bachelor and a jubilantly wedded guy to both compose

-

their tales, you'd obtain a pleasant narration from both. The solitary individual's position would nonetheless be I, me and me – and potentially a run of blind dates and Saturday evenings alone. The husband will describe "us", of joint interests — a narrative made richer as there are two stories, not one.

Much as it sounds incredibly passé, marriage is a commitment, and individuals have to make every endeavour not to diminish that relationship in any way. Remaining married is a lifetime, missionary-like activity. It calls for guts. It needs tremendous nerves of steel to make a union function. A sense of humour and a humbler degree of egotism may sustain us in that endeavour.

The blockages will be numerous, and there will be times when we'll doubt our saneness, unclear whether we may hang in there.

It will be a big effort to remain attracted to the same attributes that lured you to your spouse on the first day you were together. Your husband is nevertheless the same guy you fell in love with, he hasn't transformed his soul, his essence, simply his closet.

-

www.ingramcontent.com/pod-product-compliance
Lightning Source LLC
LaVergne TN
LVHW052105160826
845678LV00015B/3369